TAGINES & MORE

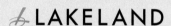 **LAKELAND**

Lakeland and Bauer Media Ltd hereby exclude all liability to the extent permitted by law for any errors or omission in this book and for any loss, damage or expense (whether direct or indirect) suffered by a third party relying on any information contained in this book.

This book was created in 2015 for Lakeland by AWW Books, an imprint of Octopus Publishing Group Ltd, based on materials licensed to it by Bauer Media Books, Sydney.

Bauer Media Limited
54 Park St, Sydney
GPO Box 4088, Sydney, NSW 2001
www.awwcookbooks.com.au

BAUER
MEDIA GROUP

OCTOPUS PUBLISHING GROUP
Design – Chris Bell
Food Director – Pamela Clark

Published for Lakeland in the United Kingdom by Octopus Publishing Group Limited

Carmelite House
50 Victoria Embankment
London EC4Y 0DZ
United Kingdom
phone + 44 (0) 207 632 5400;
fax + 44 (0) 207 632 5405
aww@octopusbooks.co.uk;
www.octopusbooks.co.uk
www.australian-womens-weekly.com

Printed and bound in China

A catalogue record for this book is available from the British Library.

ISBN 978-1-909770-30-0

The Department of Health advises that eggs should not be consumed raw. This book contains some dishes made with raw or lightly cooked eggs. It is prudent for vulnerable people such as pregnant and nursing mothers, invalids, the elderly, babies and young children to avoid uncooked or lightly cooked dishes made with eggs. Once prepared, these dishes should be kept refrigerated and used promptly.

This book also includes dishes made with nuts and nut derivatives. It is advisable for those with known allergic reactions to nuts and nut derivatives and those who may be potentially vulnerable to these allergies, such as pregnant and nursing mothers, invalids, the elderly, babies and children to avoid dishes made with nuts and nut oils. It is also prudent to check the labels of pre-prepared ingredients for the possible inclusion of nut derivatives.

Some of the recipes in this book have appeared in other publications.

TAGINES & MORE

Perfect for experienced and novice cooks alike, this collection of 55 recipes is a feast of exotic flavours. There are classic and contemporary recipes for meat, poultry and vegetarian tagines, plus an array of delicious side dishes, roasts, starters and drinks. Every recipe is accompanied by a beautiful colour photograph to inspire you to get into the kitchen and get cooking.

With every recipe triple-tested® for perfect results, this excellent cookbook is sure to be one of the best-loved on your kitchen bookshelf. To discover the rest of our range of cookbooks, together with our unrivalled selection of creative kitchenware, visit one of our friendly Lakeland stores or shop online at www.lakeland.co.uk.

Contents

NORTH AFRICAN COOKING 6

TO START 12

TAGINES 24

ROASTS 70

ACCOMPANIMENTS 82

TO DRINK 112

GLOSSARY 124

INDEX 126

CONVERSION CHARTS 128

North African cooking

A feast for the senses, the cuisine of North Africa is an intoxicating blend of spices, herbs and fresh ingredients.

The culinary traditions of North Africa interweave medieval with modern and draw on a rich heritage that combines indigenous Berber culture with Arab, Middle Eastern, Persian, Andalusian and French influences.

Sweet fruits and tangy salads, fragrant herbs and fiery spices, succulent roast meat and buttery, fluffy couscous, scented broths and comforting tagines – this is food that reflects a colourful, vibrant history of different peoples and culinary cultures that has created a magical fusion of flavours.

THE TRADITIONS

The main meal of the day is usually served at midday and begins with a series of hot and cold salads or a selection of little dishes, including perhaps a simple bowl of olives and a vegetable dip. This is followed by one or more tagines accompanied by a big platter of couscous and freshly baked bread. Meals are usually finished with fruits – such as dates, watermelon, figs and apricots – and nuts.

Steaming glasses of sweet and soothing mint tea (see the recipe on page 114) are offered as a traditional mark of hospitality and to end meals. Coffee is generally reserved for special occasions and is usually served black, spiked with aromatic cardamom seeds or cinnamon sticks. You'll find a recipe on page 122.

TAGINES

Tagine refers to the name of the unique cooking pot as well as to the wonderful, rich stews that are cooked in it. The traditional tagine pot is made of clay and consists of a round, flat base with low sides (which doubles as a serving dish) and the tall, cone-shaped lid, which acts like a closed chimney, trapping the moisture and circulating the steam and flavours during cooking.

Tagines were traditionally cooked over coals or an open flame but you can use them in your kitchen over gas flame, on an electric hob or in the oven. When using a tagine at home, follow the manufacturer's instructions. If you do not have a tagine, you can use a normal casserole dish or saucepan instead.

SOME KEY INGREDIENTS

There are some ingredients that are central to the culinary traditions of North Africa. These include:

chermoulla This appears throughout Algeria, Tunisia and Morocco. Ingredients and the quantities in which they are used vary from region to region but the predominant components are chillies, garlic, cumin seeds, lemon juice and fresh coriander. Chermoulla is used as a spicy marinade or sauce for grilled fish and poultry dishes. See page 10 for a recipe.

chickpeas Available ready to use in cans or dried, chickpeas are a key feature of North African cuisine. Crunchy and full of nutty flavour, they are a low in fat and high in fibre, vitamins and minerals, making them a healthy addition to any diet. When buying them dried, look for firm chickpeas with a uniform beige colour. Choose canned chickpeas stored in water, rather than brine. Remember that dried chickpeas need to be soaked overnight before they can be used.

couscous The staple cereal of North Africa and a vital part of culinary life, couscous is made with semolina flour mixed with water and handrolled to different sizes. Traditionally, it is prepared in a couscoussier, which is a two-tiered pot with a stewing section in the base for the meat, beans or vegetables and a steaming pot on top for the couscous.

The recipes in this book use the more familiar couscous granules that have already been steamed and dried, so they can be prepared quickly by adding boiling water or stock.

Couscous can be served warm or cold, as a side dish or mixed with other ingredients, including salad leaves, vegetables, fruit and nuts.

dukkah Originally from Egypt, this mix of coarsely ground nuts, seeds and spices is often combined with olive oil to make a dip for bread or vegetables. The traditional mix is made up of roasted hazelnuts, sesame and coriander seeds and cumin. Dried chillies, paprika, mint or thyme are often added.

harissa paste A fiery paste made from dried chillies, garlic, olive oil and spices, harissa paste can be used as a condiment on its own, as an ingredient in sauces and dressings and as a rub for meat. Blended with natural yogurt, it makes a delicious dip. Rose harissa also includes dried rose petals. It is extremely hot, so a little goes

a long way. You'll find a variety of brands to choose from at the supermarket or you can make your own – see the recipe on page 11.

preserved lemons These are speciality in North Africa and the Middle East. The lemons are preserved, whole or cut in half, in a mixture of salt and lemon juice or oil. To use, remove and discard the flesh, rinse the rind and chop or slice into tagines, couscous or dips. Preserved lemons are particularly good with lamb or fish dishes. Most big supermarkets will stock preserved lemons or you can make your own, using the recipe on page 11.

ras el hanout Translated from the Arabic as 'top of the shop', this is a blend of the best a spice merchant has to offer. It is a medley of more than 20 spices, including allspice, cumin, paprika, fennel, caraway, cinnamon and saffron. Some versions include dried rosebuds and lavender too. If you'd like to try making your own, you'll find a recipe on page 10.

split peas These are available in both green and yellow varieties

and have a sweet, strong pea flavour. They are used throughout North Africa in soups and tagines.

za'atar Originally from the Middle East, this popular blend of roasted dried thyme, oregano, marjoram, sesame seeds and sumac is found in many North African kitchens. Try it sprinkled on hummus, fried eggs or flatbreads spread with ricotta or tossed with roasted potato or sweet potato wedges.

Essential recipes

Chermoulla

125ml olive oil
80ml lemon juice
6 shallots (150g), sliced thinly
4 cloves garlic, crushed
1 teaspoon ground cumin
1 fresh red chilli, sliced thinly
3 tablespoons each finely chopped fresh coriander, mint and flat-leaf parsley

1 Combine ingredients in small bowl; season to taste.

prep + cook time 15 minutes
makes 250ml
tip This Moroccan blend of herbs and spices is traditionally used for preserving or seasoning fish or meat. It may also be used as a quick sauce for fish or seafood or as a baste or marinade.

Ras el hanout

2 teaspoons cumin seeds
1 teaspoon each caraway seeds, coriander seeds and fennel seeds
¼ teaspoon saffron threads
1 teaspoon each ground allspice, ginger, cinnamon and smoked paprika
½ teaspoon each ground turmeric, nutmeg and cardamom
¼ teaspoon each ground clove and cayenne pepper

1 Dry-fry seeds in small frying pan until fragrant; cool.
2 Crush seeds and saffron in mortar and pestle until fine. Stir in remaining spices.

prep + cook time 15 minutes
makes 3 tablespoons
tip Store in an airtight container. Stir a little ras el hanout into couscous to add colour and aroma.

Preserved lemons

10 medium lemons (1.4kg)
165g coarse cooking salt
8 whole cloves
4 cardamom pods, bruised
½ teaspoon coriander seeds
4 bay leaves
500ml lemon juice, approximately

1 Wash and dry lemons; cut into quarters lengthways. Place lemons in large bowl; sprinkle evenly with salt.
2 Pack lemons into sterilised jars with spices and bay leaves.
3 Pour in enough juice to cover lemons completely; secure lids. Stand in a cool, dry place for at least 3 weeks before using.

prep + cook time 10 minutes + 3 weeks standing
makes 1.5 litres
tip Refrigerate the preserved lemons after opening. To use lemons, remove and discard the flesh from the lemons. Chop or slice the rind and use in tagines or dips, with lamb dishes or sprinkled over fish.

Harissa paste

45g dried red chillies
2 teaspoons each cumin seeds and coriander seeds
100g roasted red pepper, chopped coarsely
3 cloves garlic, crushed
2 teaspoons sea salt
60ml extra virgin olive oil
60ml water
extra virgin olive oil, extra

1 Trim and discard chilli stems; place chillies in small heatproof bowl. Cover with boiling water; stand 1 hour. Drain.
2 Meanwhile, dry-fry seeds in small frying pan until fragrant. Cool and coarsely crush.
3 Process chillies until finely chopped. Add crushed seeds, pepper, garlic, salt, oil and the water; process until mixture forms a thick paste.
4 Spoon paste into small sterilised jars; drizzle extra oil over surface and secure lids. Refrigerate.

prep + cook time 25 minutes + standing
makes 750ml
tip Paste will keep in the fridge for up to 10 days.

To Start

Tomato & pomegranate salad **14**

Broad bean & mint dip **17**

Caraway chermoulla prawn skewers **18**

Chicken kebabs with blood orange **21**

Crispy spiced fish **22**

Tomato & pomegranate salad

1 teaspoon cumin seeds
2 medium tomatoes (300g), chopped finely
1 medium red pepper (200g), chopped finely
1 small red onion (100g), chopped finely
1 fresh red chilli, chopped finely
3 tablespoons finely chopped fresh flat-leaf
  parsley
1 tablespoon pomegranate molasses
2 tablespoons olive oil

1 Dry-fry seeds in small frying pan until fragrant; allow to cool.
2 Place seeds in medium bowl with remaining ingredients, season to taste; toss gently to combine. Serve with toasted french bread or flatbreads.

prep + cook time 20 minutes
serves 8

Broad bean & mint dip

500g frozen broad beans
1 clove garlic, crushed
1 teaspoon ground cumin
½ teaspoon smoked paprika
2 tablespoons olive oil
1 tablespoon lemon juice
1 tablespoon finely chopped fresh mint
1 tablespoon olive oil, extra
¼ teaspoon smoked paprika, extra

1 Cook beans in medium saucepan of boiling water until tender; drain, reserving some of the cooking liquid. When cool enough to handle, peel away grey-coloured outer shells from beans.
2 Blend or process beans with garlic, spices, oil, juice, mint and enough of the reserved cooking liquid until mixture is smooth.
3 Serve dip drizzled with extra oil and sprinkled with extra paprika.

prep + cook time 20 minutes
makes 435ml
tip Dip can be made a day ahead; store, covered, in the refrigerator.

Caraway chermoulla prawn skewers

16 uncooked medium king prawns (720g)
1 tablespoon olive oil
2 tablespoons each finely chopped fresh flat-leaf
    parsley, coriander and mint
2 cloves garlic, crushed
2 teaspoons finely grated lemon rind
1 tablespoon lemon juice
1 teaspoon each ground allspice and caraway seeds

1 Shell and devein prawns, leaving tails intact.
Combine prawns with oil, herbs, garlic, rind, juice,
and spices in medium bowl; season.
2 Preheat grill.
3 Thread prawns, tail-end first, onto 16 bamboo
skewers; cook prawns under grill about 5 minutes or
until changed in colour.

prep + cook time 30 minutes
makes 16
tip Soak bamboo skewers in cold water for at
least an hour before using to prevent them burning
during cooking.

Chicken kebabs with blood orange

4 medium blood oranges (960g)
8 chicken fillets (600g)
1 tablespoon moroccan seasoning
3 tablespoons finely chopped fresh flat-leaf parsley
30g finely chopped roasted unsalted shelled
   pistachios
1 tablespoon olive oil
1 tablespoon pomegranate molasses
pinch chilli powder

1 Finely grate 2 teaspoons rind from oranges.
2 Combine chicken, seasoning and rind in medium bowl; season. Thread chicken onto 8 bamboo skewers.
3 Cook kebabs on heated oiled griddle pan until chicken is cooked.
4 Meanwhile, segment oranges over small bowl; reserve 1 tablespoon juice, chop flesh finely. Combine juice and flesh with remaining ingredients in small bowl, season to taste.
5 Serve kebabs with orange mixture and, if you like, toasted flatbread.

prep + cook time 45 minutes
serves 8
tip Soak bamboo skewers in cold water for at least an hour before using to prevent them burning during cooking.

Crispy spiced fish

8 small white fish fillets (750g)
vegetable oil, for shallow-frying
2 eggs
1 teaspoon water
150g plain flour

paprika chermoulla
large handful fresh coriander leaves
1 clove garlic, crushed
1 tablespoon ground cumin
1½ teaspoons sweet paprika
pinch hot paprika
1 tablespoon olive oil
2 tablespoons water

1 Make paprika chermoulla.
2 Cut fish fillets in half. Combine fish and chermoulla in large bowl. Cover; refrigerate 2 hours or overnight.
3 Heat oil in large frying pan. Whisk eggs and the water in small shallow bowl until combined. Drain fish, then toss in flour, shake off excess. Dip fish in egg mixture, drain off excess. Shallow-fry fish, in batches, until browned lightly; drain on absorbent paper.

paprika chermoulla Blend or process ingredients until smooth; season to taste.

prep + cook time 35 minutes + refrigeration time
serves 8

Tagines

Veal, quince & caramelised onion tagine **26**

Beef & bean tagine **29**

Spicy chicken & yogurt tagine **30**

Chicken tagine with fennel & orange **33**

Chicken tagine with prunes **34**

Lamb tagine with chickpeas **37**

Lamb kefta tagine **38**

Honeyed lamb tagine **41**

Lamb tagine with baby carrots & olives **42**

Lamb, currant & quince tagine **45**

Lamb tfaya **46**

Lamb, aubergine & prune tagine **49**

Lamb chops with barley, mint & cumin **50**

Sweet potato & lamb shank tagine **53**

Tuna tagine with lentils & beans **54**

Chermoulla fish tagine **57**

Fast fish tagine **58**

White fish & tomato tagine **61**

Harissa vegetable tagine with orange & mint couscous **62**

Butternut & green bean tagine with lemon couscous **65**

Moroccan chickpea tagine **66**

Sweet pumpkin tagine with harissa & almond couscous **69**

Veal, quince & caramelised onion tagine

6 baby onions (150g)
6 thick pieces veal knuckle (1.6kg)
2 teaspoons ground ginger
2 teaspoons ground cinnamon
½ teaspoon chilli powder
1 tablespoon olive oil
1 tablespoon honey
625ml beef stock
3 cloves garlic, crushed
3 medium quinces (1kg), peeled, cored,
    cut into thick wedges
4 tablespoons coarsely chopped
    fresh coriander

1 Peel onions, leaving root ends intact; halve onions.
2 Combine veal and half the combined spices in large bowl.
3 Heat half the oil in tagine or flameproof casserole dish; cook veal, in batches, until browned. Remove from tagine.
4 Heat remaining oil in same tagine; cook onion, honey and 125ml of the stock, stirring occasionally, about 5 minutes or until onion caramelises. Remove from tagine.
5 Add garlic and remaining spices to tagine; cook, stirring, about 1 minute or until fragrant. Return veal to tagine with remaining stock and quince; bring to the boil. Reduce heat; simmer, covered, about 1½ hours or until veal is tender.
6 Add onion to tagine; simmer, covered, about 5 minutes or until heated through. Season to taste.
7 Serve tagine sprinkled with coriander and accompanied by couscous.

prep + cook time 2 hours 15 minutes
serves 6
tip Ask your butcher to cut the veal knuckle into 6 thick slices for you. You could use veal shin if you can't get veal knuckle.

Beef & bean tagine

2 tablespoons olive oil
1kg braising steak, cut into 2cm pieces
2 medium brown onions (300g), chopped
   finely
2 cloves garlic, crushed
1 teaspoon ground turmeric
2 teaspoons ground cumin
½ teaspoon dried chilli flakes
70g tomato paste
410g can chopped tomatoes
500ml beef stock
2 bay leaves
2 medium potatoes (400g), chopped coarsely
400g can kidney beans, rinsed, drained
3 tablespoons coarsely chopped fresh
   coriander
3 tablespoons coarsely chopped fresh
   flat-leaf parsley

1 Heat oil in tagine or flameproof casserole dish; cook beef, in batches, until browned.
2 Add onion and garlic to tagine; cook, stirring, until onion softens. Add spices; cook, stirring, until fragrant. Add paste; cook, stirring, 1 minute.
3 Return beef to tagine with undrained tomatoes, stock and bay leaves; bring to the boil. Reduce heat; simmer, covered, 1 hour.
4 Add potato to tagine; simmer, uncovered, about 30 minutes or until potato is tender.
5 Discard bay leaves. Add beans to tagine; stir until heated through. Remove from heat, stir through herbs.

prep + cook time 2 hours 20 minutes
serves 4

Spicy chicken & yogurt tagine

2 teaspoons ground cumin
2 teaspoons ground cardamom
1 teaspoon ground cinnamon
½ teaspoon ground clove
½ teaspoon ground turmeric
80g blanched almonds
2cm piece fresh ginger (10g), chopped coarsely
2 cloves garlic, quartered
500g natural yogurt
8 chicken thighs (1.6kg), skin removed
2 tablespoons vegetable oil
2 medium brown onions (300g), sliced thinly
80ml lemon juice
3 tablespoons finely chopped fresh coriander

1 Dry-fry spices and nuts in small heated frying pan, stirring, until nuts are browned lightly.
2 Blend or process nut mixture with ginger and garlic until mixture forms a paste. Combine mixture with yogurt in large bowl, add chicken; mix well. Cover; refrigerate 3 hours or overnight.
3 Heat oil in tagine or flameproof casserole dish; cook onion, stirring, until soft. Add chicken mixture; simmer, covered, about 45 minutes or until chicken is cooked through. Stir in juice.
4 Serve tagine sprinkled with coriander.

prep + cook time 1 hour 30 minutes + refrigeration time
serves 4

Chicken tagine with fennel & orange

1 tablespoon olive oil
20g butter
12 chicken drumsticks (1.8kg)
4 baby fennel bulbs (520g), trimmed, quartered
1 medium brown onion (150g), chopped finely
2 cloves garlic, crushed
1 tablespoon finely grated orange rind
250ml orange juice
250ml dry white wine
500ml chicken stock
6 fresh sprigs thyme
1 medium sweet potato (400g), chopped coarsely

1 Heat oil and butter in tagine or flameproof casserole dish; cook chicken, in batches, until browned. Remove from tagine. Discard all but 1 tablespoon of the juices, Reheat juices in same tagine; cook fennel in batches, until browned and caramelised, Remove from tagine.
2 Cook onion and garlic in same tagine, stirring, until onion softens. Return chicken and fennel to tagine with rind, juice, wine, stock and thyme; bring to the boil. Reduce heat; simmer, covered, about 30 minutes or until chicken is cooked.
3 Add sweet potato; simmer, uncovered, for about 20 minutes or until sweet potato is tender, Discard thyme before serving.

prep + cook time 1 hour 20 minutes
serves 4

Chicken tagine with prunes

2kg whole chicken
2 tablespoons moroccan seasoning
35g plain flour
1 tablespoon olive oil
8 shallots (200g)
170g pitted prunes, halved
120g blanched almonds, roasted
4 trimmed swiss chard leaves (320g), shredded
　　finely
500ml chicken consommé
125ml prune juice
2 tablespoons finely chopped fresh flat-leaf parsley

1 Preheat oven to 200°C/180°C fan-assisted.
2 Using kitchen scissors, cut chicken into four pieces.
3 Combine seasoning and flour in large bowl; coat chicken with flour mixture, shake off excess.
4 Heat oil in tagine or flameproof casserole dish on stove top; cook chicken, in batches, until browned. Remove from tagine; drain on absorbent paper.
5 Meanwhile, peel shallots, leaving root ends intact. Cook shallots in same heated tagine, stirring, until browned. Add prunes, nuts, half the swiss chard, consommé, juice and parsley; bring to the boil. Top with chicken.
6 Cover tagine, transfer to oven; cook about 50 minutes or until chicken is cooked. Remove from oven; stir in remaining swiss chard Season to taste. Stand tagine, covered, 10 minutes before serving.

prep + cook time 1 hour 5 minutes
serves 4
tips Ask the butcher to cut the chicken into four pieces for you, or buy four chicken leg portions. If you can't find chicken consommé, you can use chicken stock instead.

Lamb tagine with chickpeas

2 tablespoons olive oil
1.6kg diced lamb
2 medium red onions (340g), sliced thinly
3 cloves garlic, crushed
1 tablespoon ground cumin
2 teaspoons ground ginger
½ teaspoon ground turmeric
1 cinnamon stick
800g canned chopped tomatoes
750ml vegetable stock
600g canned chickpeas, rinsed, drained
3 tablespoons finely chopped fresh
   flat-leaf parsley

1 Heat half the oil in tagine or flameproof casserole dish; cook lamb, in batches, until browned. Remove from tagine.
2 Heat remaining oil in same tagine; cook onion, garlic and spices, stirring, until onion softens.
3 Return lamb to tagine with undrained tomatoes and stock; bring to the boil. Reduce heat; simmer, covered, about 1 hour or until lamb is tender. Add chickpeas; simmer, uncovered, 5 minutes. Discard cinnamon; stir in parsley, season to taste.

prep + cook time 1 hour 30 minutes
serves 6

Lamb kefta tagine

625g minced lamb
2 cloves garlic, crushed
1 medium red onion (170g), chopped finely
1 tablespoon each ground coriander, cumin and
   sweet paprika
large handful fresh coriander leaves
2 fresh small red chillies, sliced thinly
2 eggs
70g stale breadcrumbs
1 tablespoon olive oil
125ml beef stock
800g canned chopped tomatoes
150g drained sun-blush tomatoes, chopped
   coarsely
6 tablespoons fresh basil leaves, chopped coarsely

1 Preheat oven to 200°C/180°C fan-assisted.
2 Combine mince, garlic, onion, spices, coriander leaves, chilli, eggs and breadcrumbs in large bowl; season. Roll 2 heaped tablespoons of mixture into balls.
3 Heat oil in tagine or flameproof casserole dish and cook meatballs, in batches, until browned. Remove from tagine; drain meatballs on absorbent paper.
4 Return meatballs to tagine with stock, undrained tomatoes, sun-blush tomatoes and basil; bring to the boil.
5 Cover tagine, transfer to oven; cook about 35 minutes or until meatballs are cooked through. Season to taste.

prep + cook time 55 minutes
serves 4

Honeyed lamb tagine

6 lamb chump chops (800g)
1 tablespoon olive oil
2 large brown onions (400g), sliced thinly
2 cloves garlic, crushed
2 teaspoons ground cumin
1 teaspoon ground cinnamon
½ teaspoon ground ginger
pinch saffron threads
500ml water
2 small carrots (140g), chopped
2 medium courgettes (240g), chopped coarsely
300g canned chickpeas, rinsed, drained
3 teaspoons lemon juice
1 tablespoon honey

1 Trim excess fat from lamb; cut in half.
2 Heat oil in tagine or flameproof casserole dish; cook lamb, in batches, until browned. Remove from tagine.
3 Cook onion and garlic in same tagine, stirring, until soft. Add spices; cook, stirring, until fragrant. Return lamb to tagine with the water; bring to the boil. Reduce heat; simmer, covered, 20 minutes. Add carrot; simmer, covered, 10 minutes. Add courgettes, chickpeas, juice and honey; simmer, uncovered, about 15 minutes or until lamb is tender and tagine thickens slightly. Season to taste.
4 Serve lamb with couscous, if you like.

prep + cook time 1 hour 25 minutes
serves 4

Lamb tagine with baby carrots & olives

2 tablespoons olive oil
1 teaspoon ground ginger
½ teaspoon saffron threads
2kg boned lamb shoulder, chopped coarsely
2 medium brown onions (300g), sliced thinly
3 stems fresh flat-leaf parsley
3 stems fresh coriander
125ml water
500g baby carrots, trimmed
40g pitted black olives
2 tablespoons thinly sliced preserved lemon rind

1 Combine oil, ginger, saffron and lamb in large bowl.
2 Place onion and lamb mixture in tagine or flameproof casserole dish. Add herbs and the water; bring to the boil. Reduce heat; simmer, covered about 1½ hours or until lamb is tender.
3 Meanwhile, cut carrots in half lengthways and then in half crossways.
4 Remove parsley and coriander from tagine. Add carrot to tagine; simmer, uncovered, about 30 minutes or until carrots are tender.
5 Add olives and preserved lemon; simmer, uncovered, until heated through, season to taste.

prep + cook time 2 hours 25 minutes
serves 8

Lamb, currant & quince tagine

45g butter
2 tablespoons olive oil
2 medium quinces (700g), peeled, cut into thick
   wedges
90g honey
1kg boned lamb shoulder, chopped coarsely
2 tablespoons finely chopped fresh coriander stems
2 teaspoons each ground coriander and cumin
1 teaspoon ground ginger
1 cinnamon stick
375ml beef stock
2 tablespoons tomato paste
40g currants
6 tablespoons fresh coriander leaves

1 Heat butter and half the oil in tagine or flameproof casserole dish; cook quince, stirring, about 10 minutes or until browned lightly. Add half the honey; cook, stirring, about 5 minutes or until quince is lightly caramelised. Remove quince from tagine.
2 Preheat oven to 180°C/160°C fan-assisted.
3 Heat remaining oil in same tagine; cook lamb, in batches, until browned.
4 Return lamb and quince to tagine with coriander stems, spices, stock, paste and remaining honey; bring to the boil.
5 Cover tagine, transfer to oven; cook about 1½ hours or until lamb is tender.
6 Remove from oven; stir in currants and coriander leaves. Season to taste.

prep + cook time 2 hours
serves 6

Lamb tfaya

1kg boned lamb shoulder, chopped coarsely
1 tablespoon ground ginger
2 teaspoons ras el hanout
1 teaspoon ground cinnamon
2 tablespoons olive oil
1 litre water
500ml chicken stock
400g canned chickpeas, rinsed, drained
400g couscous
500ml boiling water
15g butter
3 tablespoons finely chopped fresh coriander
80g coarsely chopped blanched almonds, roasted
3 hard-boiled eggs, quartered

tfaya
2 large brown onions (400g), sliced thinly
90g honey
75g raisins
45g butter, chopped
1 teaspoon each ground white pepper and
    ground cinnamon
½ teaspoon ground turmeric
pinch saffron threads
125ml water

1 Combine lamb and spices in large bowl. Heat oil in tagine or flameproof casserole dish; cook lamb, in batches, until browned. Remove from tagine.
2 Return lamb to tagine with the water, stock and chickpeas; bring to the boil. Reduce heat; simmer, covered, 30 minutes. Uncover; simmer, stirring occasionally, about 1 hour or until lamb is tender.
3 Meanwhile, make tfaya.
4 Combine couscous, the boiling water and butter in large heatproof bowl, cover; stand about 5 minutes or until liquid is absorbed, fluffing with fork occasionally. Stir in coriander and nuts; season to taste.
5 Serve lamb mixture with couscous; accompany with tfaya and eggs.

tfaya Bring ingredients to the boil in medium saucepan. Reduce heat; simmer, uncovered, stirring occasionally, about 30 minutes or until onion is caramelised.

prep + cook time 1 hour 50 minutes
serves 6
tip Tfaya is an accompaniment of sweet and spicy caramelised onions and raisins.

Lamb, aubergine & prune tagine

2 medium aubergines (600g)
1 tablespoon coarse cooking salt
2 teaspoons sesame seeds
2 tablespoons olive oil
1kg diced lamb
1 large brown onion (200g), chopped finely
2 cloves garlic, crushed
2 teaspoons ground cumin
1 teaspoon ground turmeric
½ teaspoon ground ginger
680ml water
2 x 5cm strips lemon rind
1 cinnamon stick
125g pitted prunes, halved
80g blanched almonds, roasted
1 tablespoon honey
2 tablespoons coarsely chopped fresh coriander

1 Cut aubergines into 1cm slices, place in colander, sprinkle with salt; stand 30 minutes. Rinse under cold water; drain, then cut into quarters.
2 Dry-fry sesame seeds in tagine or large saucepan until browned lightly. Remove from tagine.
3 Heat oil in tagine; cook lamb, in batches, until browned. Remove from tagine.
4 Cook onion, garlic and spices in same tagine, stirring, until onion softens. Return lamb to tagine with the water, rind and cinnamon stick; bring to the boil. Reduce heat; simmer, covered, about 1 hour or until lamb is tender.
5 Add prunes, nuts, honey, coriander and aubergines; simmer, covered, about 30 minutes or until aubergines are tender. Discard cinnamon stick and rind; season tagine to taste. Serve sprinkled with sesame seeds.

prep + cook time 2 hours
serves 6

Lamb chops with barley, mint & cumin

1 tablespoon olive oil
8 lamb chops or leg steaks (1.5kg)
20g butter
1 large brown onion (200g), chopped coarsely
2 cloves garlic, chopped finely
1 tablespoon ground cumin
2 large red peppers (700g), chopped coarsely
200g pearl barley
2 teaspoons finely grated orange rind
250ml orange juice
1 litre chicken stock
500ml water
3 tablespoons fresh mint leaves

1 Heat oil in tagine or flameproof casserole dish; cook lamb, in batches, until browned all over.
2 Heat butter in same tagine; cook onion and garlic, stirring, until onion softens. Add cumin and pepper; cook, stirring, until fragrant.
3 Return lamb to tagine with barley, rind, juice, stock and the water; bring to the boil. Reduce heat; simmer, covered, for 45 minutes. Uncover; simmer for 30 minutes or until lamb is tender.
4 Strain mixture over a large bowl; cover lamb mixture to keep warm. Return cooking liquid to tagine; bring to the boil. Boil, uncovered, stirring occasionally, for 15 minutes or until sauce thickens slightly.
5 Return meat to tagine and serve sprinkled with mint.

prep + cook time 2 hours 15 minutes
serves 4

Sweet potato & lamb shank tagine

8 french-trimmed lamb shanks (2kg)
2 tablespoons plain flour
60ml olive oil
2 medium brown onions (300g), chopped coarsely
3 cloves garlic, crushed
1 teaspoon ground cinnamon
2 teaspoons ground cumin
2 teaspoons ground coriander
250ml dry red wine
1 litre chicken stock
2 tablespoons honey
2 small sweet potatoes (500g), chopped coarsely

olive & almond couscous
300g couscous
375ml boiling water
20g butter
2 tablespoons finely chopped preserved lemon
90g pitted green olives, chopped coarsely
4 tablespoons coarsely chopped fresh flat-leaf
    parsley
45g roasted flaked almonds
1 medium green pepper (200g), chopped finely

1 Preheat oven to 180°C/160°C fan-assisted.
2 Toss lamb in flour; shake away excess. Heat 2 tablespoons of the oil in tagine or flameproof casserole dish; cook lamb, in batches, until browned all over. Drain on absorbent paper.
3 Heat remaining oil in same tagine; cook onion, garlic, cinnamon, cumin and coriander, stirring, until onion softens and mixture is fragrant. Add wine; bring to a boil. Simmer, uncovered, about 5 minutes or until liquid reduces by half.
4 Add stock and honey to same tagine; bring to a boil. Return lamb to tagine; cook, covered, in oven, about 1½ hours, turning shanks occasionally. Uncover, add sweet potato; return to oven. Cook, uncovered, about 50 minutes or until potato is just tender and lamb is almost falling off the bone. Transfer lamb and potato to platter; cover to keep warm.
5 Place tagine with juices over high heat; bring to a boil. Boil, uncovered, about 15 minutes or until sauce thickens slightly. Return lamb and potato to tagine.
6 Meanwhile, make olive and almond couscous.
7 Serve tagine with couscous.

olive & almond couscous Combine couscous with the water and butter in large heatproof bowl, cover; stand about 5 minutes or until liquid is absorbed, fluffing with fork occasionally. Stir in remaining ingredients.

prep + cook time 3 hour 15 minutes
serves 4

Tuna tagine with lentils & beans

4 x 185g tuna steaks
2 teaspoons each ground coriander and cumin
½ teaspoon dried chilli flakes
60ml olive oil
4 tablespoons finely chopped fresh flat-leaf parsley
2 large carrots (360g), cut into matchsticks
500ml chicken consommé
1 tablespoon honey
800g canned brown lentils, rinsed, drained
90g frozen broad beans, thawed, peeled
1 tablespoon coarsely chopped fresh flat-leaf
   parsley, extra

1 Combine tuna, spices, chilli, half the oil and half the parsley in large bowl. Cover, refrigerate 3 hours or overnight.
2 Heat remaining oil in tagine or flameproof casserole dish; cook carrots, stirring, until tender. Add consommé, honey, lentils and half the beans; top with tuna. Bring to the boil, reduce heat; simmer, covered, about 10 minutes or until tuna is cooked as desired. Season to taste.
3 Stir in remaining beans; stand tagine, covered, 5 minutes. Serve sprinkled with extra parsley.

prep + cook time 30 minutes + refrigeration time
serves 4
tips Ask your fishmonger to cut thick tuna steaks; thin steaks can easily overcook and dry out. If you can't find chicken consommé, you can use chicken stock instead.

Chermoulla fish tagine

4 x 200g white fish fillets, skin on
60ml olive oil
500g small red-skinned potatoes, unpeeled,
 sliced thickly
500g cherry tomatoes on the vine
125ml chicken stock
2 tablespoons tomato paste
1 teaspoon granulated sugar
3 tablespoons each fresh flat-leaf parsley leaves
 and mint leaves

harissa chermoulla
3 tablespoons each coarsely chopped fresh flat-leaf
 parsley and coriander
2 tablespoons lemon juice
1 tablespoon olive oil
2 cloves garlic, halved
2 teaspoons each ground cumin and sweet paprika
2 teaspoons harissa paste

1 Make chermoulla.
2 Combine fish and chermoulla in large bowl.
Cover; refrigerate 30 minutes.
3 Heat half the oil in tagine or flameproof casserole
dish; cook potato, stirring, about 10 minutes or
until browned lightly. Cover; cook 5 minutes or until
potatoes are almost tender.
4 Uncover potatoes; top with fish and tomatoes.
Combine stock, tomato paste and sugar in medium
jug; season to taste. Pour stock mixture over fish
in tagine; bring to the boil. Reduce heat; simmer,
covered, about 20 minutes or until fish is cooked.
5 Serve tagine drizzled with remaining oil; sprinkle
with herbs.

harissa chermoulla Blend or process ingredients
until almost smooth.

prep + cook time 50 minutes + refrigeration time
serves 4
tips You can use any white fish fillets in this recipe.
We used desiree potatoes in this recipe.

Fast fish tagine

4 x 200g firm white fish fillets, skin on, halved crossways
2 tablespoons moroccan seasoning
2 tablespoons olive oil
1 large brown onion (200g), sliced thinly
3 cloves garlic, crushed
1 medium lemon (140g), sliced thinly
12 pitted green olives (95g)
250ml chicken stock
1 teaspoon granulated sugar
2 tablespoons coarsely chopped fresh coriander

herb couscous
200g couscous
250ml boiling water
6 tablespoons fresh coriander leaves

1 Preheat oven to 200°C/180°C fan-assisted.
2 Combine fish and seasoning in large bowl.
3 Heat half the oil in tagine or flameproof casserole dish; cook onion and garlic, stirring, until soft. Remove from tagine and set aside. Heat the remaining oil in same tagine; cook fish, in batches, until browned. Return onion mixture to the tagine with lemon, olives, stock and sugar; bring to the boil.
4 Transfer tagine to oven; cook, uncovered, about 10 minutes or until fish is cooked, season to taste.
5 Meanwhile, make herb couscous.
6 Sprinkle tagine with coriander; serve with herb couscous and steamed courgette slices, if you like.

herb couscous Combine couscous and the water in medium heatproof bowl, cover; stand 5 minutes or until liquid is absorbed, fluffing with fork occasionally. Stir in coriander.

prep + cook time 30 minutes
serves 4

White fish & tomato tagine

2 tablespoons olive oil
2 large brown onions (400g), chopped coarsely
6 cloves garlic, chopped finely
1 fresh small red chilli, chopped finely
4 drained anchovy fillets, chopped finely
large handful coarsely chopped fresh coriander
handful each coarsely chopped fresh flat-leaf parsley and mint
200g button mushrooms, quartered
2 stalks celery (300g), trimmed, sliced thickly
2 teaspoons ground cumin
850g canned chopped tomatoes
4 x 250g firm white fish cutlets
1 medium lemon (140g), cut into wedges
2 tablespoons fresh flat-leaf parsley leaves

1 Preheat oven to 200°C/180°C fan-assisted.
2 Heat oil in tagine or large flameproof baking dish; cook onion, garlic and chilli, stirring, until onion softens. Add anchovy, chopped herbs, mushrooms, celery and cumin; cook, stirring, 5 minutes.
3 Add undrained tomatoes; bring to the boil. Add fish; return to the boil. Transfer tagine to oven; cook, uncovered, about 20 minutes or until liquid has almost evaporated and fish is cooked as desired.
4 Divide fish and lemon wedges among serving plates; sprinkle with parsley. Serve tagine with a tomato and herb salad and steamed long-grain white rice, if you like.

prep + cook time 1 hour
serves 4

Harissa vegetable tagine with orange & mint couscous

2 medium carrots (240g)
2 medium courgettes (240g)
2 small leeks (400g)
1 teaspoon olive oil
1 medium brown onion (150g), chopped finely
1 clove garlic, crushed
1 stalk celery (150g), trimmed, chopped coarsely
3 teaspoons harissa paste
1 tablespoon tomato paste
425g canned chopped tomatoes
310ml water
1 tablespoon orange juice
20g roasted flaked almonds

orange & mint couscous
300g couscous
1 teaspoon olive oil
375ml boiling water
2 teaspoons finely grated orange rind
1 tablespoon orange juice
2 tablespoons coarsely chopped fresh mint

1 Preheat oven to 180°C/160°C fan-assisted.
2 Quarter carrots and courgettes lengthways; cut into 4cm lengths. Halve leeks lengthways; cut into 6cm lengths.
3 Heat oil in tagine or flameproof casserole dish; cook onion and garlic, stirring, until onion softens. Add carrot, courgette, leek, celery, harissa paste, tomato paste, undrained tomatoes and the water; bring to the boil. Cover tagine, transfer to oven; cook about 40 minutes or until vegetables are tender. Remove from oven; stir in juice, season to taste.
4 Meanwhile, make orange and mint couscous.
5 Divide couscous and tagine among serving bowls; sprinkle with nuts.

orange & mint couscous Combine couscous, oil and the water in medium heatproof bowl, cover; stand about 5 minutes or until liquid is absorbed, fluffing with fork occasionally. Stir in remaining ingredients.

prep + cook time 1 hour 10 minutes
serves 4

Butternut & green bean tagine with lemon couscous

1 tablespoon each coriander seeds, cumin seeds
  and caraway seeds
1 tablespoon vegetable oil
3 cloves garlic, crushed
2 large brown onions (400g), chopped finely
2 teaspoons each sweet paprika and ground ginger
1 tablespoon tomato paste
500ml water
800g canned chopped tomatoes
600g butternut squash, chopped coarsely
8 yellow patty pan squash (240g), quartered
200g fine green beans, trimmed, halved
300g canned chickpeas, rinsed, drained

lemon couscous
400g couscous
500ml boiling water
2 teaspoons coarsely grated lemon rind
2 teaspoons lemon juice
2 tablespoons coarsely chopped fresh flat-leaf
  parsley

1 Using mortar and pestle, crush seeds to a fine powder. Sift into small bowl; discard husks.
2 Heat oil in a tagine or flameproof casserole dish; cook garlic and onion, stirring, until onion softens. Add crushed seeds and spices; cook, stirring, until fragrant.
3 Add paste, the water, undrained tomatoes and butternut squash; bring to the boil. Reduce heat; simmer, uncovered, 20 minutes. Stir in patty pan squash, beans and chickpeas; simmer, covered, about 10 minutes or until squash is tender, season to taste.
4 Meanwhile, make lemon couscous.
5 Serve tagine with couscous.

lemon couscous Combine couscous with the water in large heatproof bowl, cover; stand about 5 minutes or until liquid is absorbed, fluffing with fork occasionally. Stir in rind, juice and parsley.

prep + cook time 1 hour 5 minutes
serves 6
tip If you can't find patty pan squash, you can increase the quantity of butternut squash instead, adding all of it to the cooker at the same time.

Moroccan chickpea tagine

1 tablespoon olive oil
1 large red onion (300g), sliced thinly
3 cloves garlic, crushed
1 fresh long red chilli, chopped finely
2 tablespoons moroccan seasoning
pinch saffron threads
1.2kg canned chickpeas, rinsed, drained
1 large carrot (180g), halved, sliced thickly
½ medium cauliflower (750g), cut into large florets
400g canned chopped tomatoes
750ml vegetable or chicken stock
1 tablespoon honey
250g cavolo nero, trimmed, shredded coarsely
250g yellow patty pan squash, halved
1 tablespoon Greek-style yogurt
2 tablespoons finely sliced preserved lemon rind
4 tablespoons fresh flat-leaf parsley leaves

1 Preheat oven to 180°C/160°C fan-assisted.
2 Heat oil in a tagine or flameproof casserole dish over low heat; cook onion, garlic and chilli, stirring, until onion softens.
3 Add seasoning and saffron to tagine; cook, stirring, for 1 minute. Add chickpeas, carrot, cauliflower, tomatoes, stock and honey; bring to the boil.
4 Cover tagine, transfer to oven; cook for 30 minutes or until vegetables are tender.
5 Add cavolo nero and squash to tagine; return to oven. Cook, covered, for 5 minutes or until squash is tender. Season to taste.
6 Serve topped with yogurt and sprinkled with preserved lemon rind and parsley.

prep + cook time 50 minutes
serves 4
tip If you can't find patty pan squash, you can use 250g butternut squash instead, adding it to the cooker at the same time as the other vegetables in step 3.

Sweet pumpkin tagine with harissa & almond couscous

20g butter
1 tablespoon olive oil
2 medium brown onions (300g), chopped coarsely
2 cloves garlic, crushed
4cm piece fresh ginger (20g), grated
2 teaspoons each ground coriander and cumin
2 teaspoons finely grated lemon rind
1kg pumpkin, chopped coarsely
400g canned chopped tomatoes
500ml vegetable stock
400g green beans, trimmed, cut into 5cm lengths
55g sultanas
1 tablespoon honey
3 tablespoons each finely chopped fresh flat-leaf
    parsley and mint

harissa & almond couscous
500ml vegetable stock
250ml water
600g couscous
70g chopped almonds, roasted
1 tablespoon harissa paste

1 Heat butter and oil in tagine or flameproof casserole dish; cook onion and garlic, stirring, 5 minutes. Add ginger, spices and rind; cook, stirring, about 1 minute or until fragrant. Add pumpkin, undrained tomatoes and stock; bring to the boil. Reduce heat; simmer, covered, about 15 minutes or until pumpkin is tender.
2 Meanwhile, make harissa & almond couscous.
3 Add beans to tagine; cook, stirring, 5 minutes. Remove from heat; stir in sultanas, honey and herbs, season to taste.
4 Serve tagine with couscous.

harissa & almond couscous Bring stock and the water to the boil in medium saucepan. Combine couscous and hot stock mixture in large heatproof bowl, cover; stand about 5 minutes or until liquid is absorbed, fluffing with fork occasionally. Stir in almonds and harissa paste.

prep + cook time 1 hour
serves 6

Roasts

Roast chicken with fruity couscous stuffing **72**

Harissa & orange-roasted chicken with baby vegetables **75**

Beef fillet with chermoulla **76**

Lamb with minted couscous **79**

Sardines with preserved lemon salsa **80**

Roast chicken with fruity couscous stuffing

100g couscous
125ml boiling water
2 tablespoons honey
½ teaspoon each ground coriander and cumin
¼ teaspoon ground cinnamon
2 tablespoons each coarsely chopped raisins
    and dried apricots
1.6kg whole chicken
80ml orange juice
1 teaspoon dried oregano
½ teaspoon sweet paprika
250ml water

orange honey yogurt
200g natural yogurt
2 teaspoons honey
1 teaspoon finely grated orange rind

1 Preheat oven to 200°C/180°C fan-assisted.
2 Combine couscous with the boiling water and honey in small heatproof bowl, cover; stand about 5 minutes or until liquid is absorbed, fluffing with fork occasionally. Stir in spices and fruit, season to taste.
3 Tuck wing tips under chicken. Trim skin around neck; secure neck flap to underside of chicken with skewers. Fill cavity with couscous mixture, fold skin to enclose stuffing; secure with skewers. Tie legs together with kitchen string.
4 Place chicken in oiled medium baking dish. Drizzle chicken with juice, sprinkle with oregano and paprika; pour the water into dish. Season. Roast chicken about 1½ hours, basting occasionally with juices, or until chicken is cooked.
5 Meanwhile, combine ingredients for orange honey yogurt in small bowl.
6 Serve chicken with stuffing and yogurt.

prep + cook time 1 hour 50 minutes
serves 4

Harissa & orange-roasted chicken with baby vegetables

1.6kg whole chicken
1 small orange (180g), cut into thin wedges
1 tablespoon olive oil
300g baby onions
500g baby new potatoes
1 bulb garlic, separated into cloves
4 baby aubergines (240g), halved lengthways
250g cherry tomatoes

orange harissa paste
15g dried red chillies, chopped coarsely
½ teaspoon each ground coriander, cumin
   and caraway seeds
1 clove garlic, quartered
1 tablespoon tomato paste
2 teaspoons finely grated orange rind
60ml orange juice

1 Preheat oven to 180°C/160°C fan-assisted.
2 Make orange harissa paste.
3 Tuck wing tips under chicken. Fill large cavity with orange. Make a pocket between breast and skin with fingers; rub 2 tablespoons of the harissa paste under skin inside pocket. Tie legs together with kitchen string; brush chicken all over with 2 tablespoons of the harissa paste.
4 Half-fill large shallow baking dish with water; place chicken on oiled wire rack over dish, season. Roast, uncovered, about 1 hour.
5 Meanwhile, heat oil in large flameproof baking dish; cook onions, potatoes and unpeeled garlic, stirring, until vegetables are browned.
6 Cover chicken; roast about 50 minutes or until chicken is cooked through. Add aubergines and tomatoes to vegetable mixture in dish, season; place in oven for about the last 20 minutes of chicken cooking time or until vegetables are tender.
7 Serve chicken with roasted vegetables and remaining harissa paste.

orange harissa paste Place chilli in small heatproof bowl of boiling water; stand 1 hour. Drain; reserve 60ml soaking liquid. Dry-fry spices in small frying pan until fragrant. Blend or process spices, chilli, reserved soaking liquid, garlic and paste until mixture is smooth; transfer to small bowl, stir in rind and juice.

prep + cook time 2 hours 35 minutes + standing time
serves 4

Beef fillet with chermoulla

2 teaspoons grated lemon rind
1 tablespoon lemon juice
2 teaspoons sweet paprika
1 teaspoon each ground coriander and cumin
3 tablespoons coarsely chopped fresh flat-leaf
  parsley
2 tablespoons coarsely chopped fresh
  coriander
2 tablespoons olive oil
700g piece fillet of beef

1 Preheat oven to 200°C/180°C fan-assisted.
2 Combine rind, juice, spices, herbs and oil in large bowl.
3 Tie beef with kitchen string at 2cm intervals; rub beef all over with herb mixture, season. Place beef on oiled wire rack over large baking shallow dish.
4 Roast, uncovered, about 30 minutes or until cooked as desired. Stand, covered, 10 minutes; remove string then slice thinly.
5 Serve beef with lemon wedges, if desired.

prep + cook time 45 minutes + standing time
serves 4
tip The beef can be marinated for two hours, if you prefer. It is best cooked close to serving.

Lamb with minted couscous

1.3 kg lamb leg joint
handful fresh mint leaves
70g natural yogurt
1 tablespoon ground cumin
½ teaspoon ground allspice
2 tablespoons lemon juice
250ml water

minted couscous
500g couscous
500ml boiling water
60g butter
100g coarsely chopped pitted prunes
70g chopped almonds, roasted
40g sliced pitted black olives
2 tablespoons coarsely chopped fresh mint

1 Place lamb in large shallow dish. Blend or process mint, yogurt, spices and juice until smooth. Pour mint mixture over lamb, turn to coat well; season. Cover; refrigerate 30 minutes or overnight.
2 Preheat oven to 180°C/160°C fan-assisted.
3 Place lamb on oiled wire rack over large baking dish; pour the water into dish. Roast, uncovered, about 1½ hours or until lamb is tender. Cover loosely with foil; stand 15 minutes before slicing thinly.
4 Meanwhile, make minted couscous.
5 Serve lamb with couscous.

minted couscous Combine couscous, the water and butter in medium heatproof bowl, cover; stand about 5 minutes or until liquid is absorbed, fluffy with fork occasionally. Stir in remaining ingredients; season to taste.

prep + cook time 2 hours + refrigeration time
serves 6

Sardines with preserved lemon salsa

2 tablespoons olive oil
1 medium brown onion (150g), chopped finely
6 drained anchovy fillets
2 cloves garlic, crushed
500g cherry tomatoes
800g canned chopped tomatoes
90g pitted black olives, chopped coarsely
3 tablespoons coarsely chopped fresh flat-leaf
   parsley
12 butterflied sardines (400g)

preserved lemon salsa
handful coarsely chopped fresh flat-leaf parsley
50g finely chopped preserved lemon rind
1 clove garlic, crushed
2 tablespoons olive oil

1 Preheat oven to 220°C/200°C fan-assisted.
2 Heat oil in medium saucepan; cook onion, anchovy and garlic, stirring, until onion softens. Add cherry tomatoes, undrained canned tomatoes, olives and parsley; bring to the boil.
3 Pour tomato mixture into medium baking dish. Place sardines, skin-side up, over tomato mixture; season. Roast, uncovered, in oven about 15 minutes or until sardines are cooked.
4 Meanwhile, make preserved lemon salsa.
5 Serve sardine mixture topped with salsa.

preserved lemon salsa Combine ingredients in small bowl.

prep + cook time 40 minutes
serves 4
tip Whiting fillets could be used instead of sardines. Ask your fishmonger to butterfly the sardines for you.

Accompaniments

Baked tomato couscous **84**

Saffron cinnamon couscous **87**

Fennel & tomato couscous **88**

Olive & parsley couscous **91**

Roasted pumpkin & spinach couscous **92**

Couscous with tomato & rocket **95**

Moroccan orange & radish salad **96**

Tomato, olive & radish salad **99**

Olive, chickpea & spinach couscous salad **100**

Sumac, onion & mint salad **103**

Tomato & preserved lemon salad **104**

Honey-spiced carrots & sweet potatoes **107**

Baked cabbage with tomatoes **108**

Aubergine & pepper with preserved lemon **111**

Baked tomato couscous

250ml chicken stock
200g couscous
15g butter
2 trimmed medium swiss chard leaves (160g),
    shredded finely
410g tomato purée
60g coarsely grated gruyère cheese

1 Preheat oven to 200°C/180°C fan-assisted.
Oil shallow 1-litre ovenproof dish.
2 Bring stock to the boil in medium saucepan;
remove from heat, add couscous and butter.
Cover; stand about 5 minutes or until liquid is
absorbed, fluffing with fork occasionally. Stir
swiss chard into couscous; season to taste.
3 Spoon couscous into dish; press down
gently. Pour tomato over couscous, sprinkle
with cheese.
4 Bake about 30 minutes or until cheese is
browned lightly.

prep + cook time 45 minutes
serves 6

Saffron cinnamon couscous

875ml chicken stock
1 teaspoon saffron threads
4 cinnamon sticks
600g couscous
2 tablespoons vegetable oil
2 medium red onions (340g), chopped finely
3 cloves garlic, crushed
2 small fresh red chillies, chopped finely
2 teaspoons ground cumin
105g slivered almonds, roasted
large handful coarsely chopped fresh coriander

1 Bring stock, saffron and cinnamon to the boil in small saucepan. Reduce heat; simmer, covered, 15 minutes. Remove cinnamon sticks.
2 Combine couscous and hot stock in large heatproof bowl, cover; stand about 5 minutes or until liquid is absorbed, fluffing with fork occasionally.
3 Meanwhile, heat oil in large frying pan; cook onion, garlic, chilli and cumin, stirring, until onion softens.
4 Add couscous to pan; stir until heated through. Stir in nuts and coriander; season to taste.

prep + cook time 20 minutes
serves 8
tip This recipe is best made close to serving time.

Fennel & tomato couscous

250g cherry tomatoes, halved
cooking-oil spray
200g couscous
250ml boiling water
2 baby fennel bulbs (260g), trimmed, sliced thinly
60ml olive oil
1 tablespoon white wine vinegar
1 clove garlic, crushed
2 tablespoons finely chopped fresh oregano

1 Preheat oven to 200°C/180°C fan-assisted.
2 Place tomatoes on oven tray; spray with cooking oil. Roast about 10 minutes or until skins burst.
3 Meanwhile, combine couscous and the water in medium heatproof bowl, cover; stand about 5 minutes or until liquid is absorbed, fluffing with fork occasionally.
4 Stir tomato and remaining ingredients into couscous.

prep + cook time 20 minutes
serves 4

Olive & parsley couscous

375ml vegetable stock
300g couscous
30g butter
120g pitted black olives
6 tablespoons coarsely chopped fresh flat-leaf
  parsley

1 Bring stock to the boil in small saucepan.
2 Combine couscous, butter and hot stock in large heatproof bowl, cover; stand about 5 minutes or until liquid is absorbed, fluffing with fork occasionally.
3 Stir olives and parsley into couscous; season to taste.

prep + cook time 15 minutes
serves 4

Roasted pumpkin & spinach couscous

600g pumpkin, chopped coarsely
1 tablespoon olive oil
250ml chicken stock
250ml water
400g couscous
150g trimmed spinach, shredded coarsely
50g walnuts, chopped coarsely

cumin dressing
60ml lemon juice
60ml olive oil
1 teaspoon honey
¾ teaspoon ground cumin
½ teaspoon cayenne pepper

1 Preheat oven to 220°C/200°C fan-assisted.
2 Place pumpkin, in single layer, on oven tray; drizzle with oil. Roast about 30 minutes or until tender, turning halfway through cooking time.
3 Meanwhile, bring stock and the water to the boil in medium saucepan. Combine couscous and hot stock mixture in large heatproof bowl, cover; stand 5 minutes, fluffing with fork occasionally. Stir in spinach, cover; stand 5 minutes.
4 Make cumin dressing.
5 Stir pumpkin, nuts and dressing into couscous mixture.

cumin dressing Place ingredients in screw-top jar, season to taste; shake well.

prep + cook time 45 minutes
serves 4

tip You need about 300g of untrimmed spinach for this recipe. If you are using baby spinach leaves, they won't need trimming so you will need 150g.

Couscous with tomato & rocket

2 teaspoons olive oil
1 large red onion (300g), chopped finely
1 clove garlic, crushed
400g couscous
45g butter
500ml boiling water
4 medium tomatoes (600g), chopped coarsely
80g pine nuts, roasted
100g rocket leaves, chopped coarsely
2 tablespoons finely chopped fresh basil
1 tablespoon finely chopped fresh flat-parsley
1 tablespoon finely grated lemon rind
60ml extra virgin olive oil
2 tablespoons lemon juice

1 Heat oil in small frying pan; cook onion and garlic, stirring, until onion softens.
2 Combine couscous, butter and the water in large heatproof bowl, cover; stand about 5 minutes or until liquid is absorbed, fluffing with fork occasionally. Cool.
3 Stir onion mixture and remaining ingredients into couscous; season to taste.

prep + cook time 20 minutes
serves 4

Moroccan orange & radish salad

10 trimmed medium radishes (150g),
   sliced thinly
4 large oranges (1.2kg), segmented
1 small red onion (100g), sliced thinly
2 tablespoons coarsely chopped fresh
   flat-leaf parsley
2 tablespoons coarsely chopped fresh
   coriander
60ml orange juice

1 Assemble radish, orange and onion on serving platter; sprinkle with parsley and coriander, drizzle with juice.
2 Cover salad; refrigerate 1 hour before serving.

prep + cook time 20 minutes + refrigeration time
serves 4

Tomato, olive & radish salad

200g pitted black olives
200g red baby plum tomatoes, halved
14 trimmed radishes (210g), sliced thinly
200g button mushrooms, halved
6 tablespoons fresh flat-leaf parsley leaves

moroccan dressing
2 teaspoons moroccan seasoning
½ teaspoon each ground coriander and
   sweet paprika
2 tablespoons red wine vinegar
80ml extra virgin olive oil

1 Make moroccan dressing.
2 Combine salad ingredients and dressing in large bowl. Cover; refrigerate 3 hours before serving.

moroccan dressing Place ingredients in screw-top jar; shake well.

prep + cook time 15 minutes + refrigeration time
serves 8
tip Salad can be prepared a day ahead; add the dressing up to 3 hours before serving.

Olive, chickpea & spinach couscous salad

300g couscous
375ml boiling water
20g butter
420g canned chickpeas, rinsed, drained
55g sultanas
50g roasted pine nuts
100g rocket leaves, chopped coarsely
handful finely chopped fresh flat-leaf parsley
120g pitted green olives

preserved lemon dressing
1 tablespoon finely grated lemon rind
60ml lemon juice
60ml olive oil
2 tablespoons finely chopped preserved lemon rind

1 Combine couscous and the water in large heatproof bowl, cover; stand about 5 minutes or until liquid is absorbed, fluffing with fork occasionally. Stir in butter. Stand 10 minutes.
2 Meanwhile, make preserved lemon dressing.
3 Stir dressing and remaining ingredients into couscous.

preserved lemon dressing Place ingredients in screw-top jar, season to taste; shake well.

prep + cook time 20 minutes
serves 4

Sumac, onion & mint salad

4 small red onions (400g), sliced thinly
2 tablespoons olive oil
2 tablespoons finely chopped fresh mint
1 tablespoon lemon juice
1 tablespoon sumac

1 Combine ingredients in medium bowl; season to taste.

prep + cook time 10 minutes
serves 8
tip Any small mint leaves can be left whole, rather than chopped.

Tomato & preserved lemon salad

750g small plum tomatoes, halved
1 small red onion (100g), sliced thinly
6 tablespoons fresh coriander leaves

preserved lemon & parsley dressing
80ml lemon juice
2 tablespoons olive oil
1 tablespoon finely chopped preserved lemon rind
1 tablespoon finely chopped fresh flat-leaf parsley
1 clove garlic, crushed
½ teaspoon granulated sugar
¼ teaspoon ground cumin
pinch sweet paprika

1 Make preserved lemon dressing.
2 Combine tomato, onion, coriander and dressing in large bowl; season to taste.

preserved lemon & parsley dressing Place ingredients in screw-top jar; shake well.

prep + cook time 10 minutes
serves 6

Honey-spiced carrots & sweet potatoes

4 medium carrots (480g)
2 small sweet potatoes (500g), sliced thickly
45g butter, melted
1 tablespoon olive oil
1½ teaspoons ground cumin
1 teaspoon cumin seeds
90g honey
2 tablespoons coarsely chopped fresh flat-leaf parsley

1 Preheat oven to 220°C/200°C fan-assisted.
2 Cut carrots into 4cm pieces. Cook carrot and sweet potatoes in large saucepan of boiling water 5 minutes; drain.
3 Combine butter, oil, cumin, seeds and honey in small bowl. Place vegetables on oiled wire rack over large baking dish. Brush vegetables with honey-spice mixture. Roast, uncovered, about 20 minutes, brushing with remaining honey-spice mixture, until vegetables are tender.
4 Serve vegetables sprinkled with parsley.

prep + cook time 45 minutes
serves 4

Baked cabbage with tomatoes

400g canned chopped tomatoes
1 small brown onion (80g), grated coarsely
1 clove garlic, crushed
1 teaspoon ground cumin
½ teaspoon granulated sugar
2 baby green cabbages (800g), quartered
2 tablespoons olive oil
2 tablespoons coarsely chopped fresh flat-leaf
  parsley

1 Preheat oven to 160°C/140°C fan-assisted.
2 Combine undrained tomatoes, onion, garlic, cumin and sugar in small bowl; season to taste.
3 Place cabbage in medium ovenproof dish; top with tomato mixture. Bake, covered, about 30 minutes or until cabbage is tender.
4 Serve cabbage mixture drizzled with oil; sprinkle with parsley.

prep + cook time 40 minutes
serves 6
tip If you can't find baby cabbage, use 1 small green cabbage and cut into eight wedges.

Aubergine & pepper with preserved lemon

3 medium aubergines (900g)
1 medium red pepper (200g)
vegetable oil, for shallow-frying
2 cloves garlic, unpeeled
1 tablespoon finely chopped preserved lemon rind
1 teaspoon each ground cumin and sweet paprika
1 tablespoon finely chopped fresh flat-leaf parsley

1 Using vegetable peeler, remove about half the skin from the aubergine in strips. Cut the aubergine into 1cm slices.
2 Preheat grill.
3 Quarter pepper; discard seeds and membranes. Cook under grill, skin-side up, until skin blisters and blackens. Cover pepper in cling film or greaseproof paper for 5 minutes; peel away skin, chop finely.
4 Heat oil with garlic in large frying pan; shallow-fry aubergine, in batches, until browned lightly; drain on absorbent paper. Discard garlic.
5 Chop aubergine coarsely; combine aubergine with pepper, preserved lemon, cumin and paprika, season to taste. Serve sprinkled with parsley.

prep + cook time 50 minutes
serves 6

To drink

Mint tea **114**

Green apple & rosewater milk **117**

Almond milk **118**

Citrus sparkler **121**

Spiced coffee with rosewater cream **122**

Mint tea

1.25 litres boiling water
large handful fresh mint leaves
55g demerara sugar
15g green tea leaves

1 Combine 250ml of the water and two-thirds of the mint in medium heatproof jug; drain, reserve mint.
2 Stir drained mint, the remaining water, sugar and tea in medium saucepan over heat until sugar dissolves. Bring to the boil.
3 Strain tea into large heatproof jug.
4 Serve heatproof glasses of tea topped with remaining mint.

prep + cook time 15 minutes
makes 1.25 litres

Green apple & rosewater milk

4 medium green-skinned apples (600g),
   peeled, cored, chopped coarsely
½ teaspoon rosewater
500ml milk
2 tablespoons caster sugar

1 Process ingredients until smooth.
2 Strain mixture into large jug; serve over ice.

prep + cook time 15 minutes
makes 1 litre

Almond milk

320g blanched almonds
500ml buttermilk
500ml milk
75g caster sugar
½ teaspoon orange blossom water
pinch ground nutmeg

1 Blend nuts, buttermilk and half the milk until smooth.
2 Stir remaining milk and sugar in small saucepan over heat until sugar dissolves. Cool.
3 Combine almond mixture and milk mixture in large jug; stir in orange blossom water. Refrigerate 3 hours or until required.
4 Serve almond milk over ice; sprinkle with nutmeg.

prep + cook time 20 minutes + refrigeration time
makes 1.5 litres

Citrus sparkler

160ml each strained lemon, orange and
   pink grapefruit juice
110g caster sugar
½ teaspoon orange blossom water
1 small pink grapefruit (350g), quartered,
   sliced thinly
6 tablespoons fresh mint leaves
1.25 litres chilled sparkling mineral water

1 Stir juices and sugar in large jug until sugar
dissolves.
2 Stir in remaining ingredients. Serve over ice.

prep + cook time 20 minutes
makes 1.5 litres

Spiced coffee with rosewater cream

8 cardamom pods
3 cinnamon sticks
4 cloves
30g instant coffee granules
1 litre water
55g light brown sugar
80ml single cream
1 teaspoon rosewater

1 Dry-fry spices in small frying pan until fragrant.
2 Combine spices, coffee, the water and sugar in medium saucepan; stir over heat until sugar dissolves. Bring to the boil. Reduce heat; simmer, stirring occasionally, 10 minutes.
3 Meanwhile, lightly beat cream and rosewater in small bowl with electric mixer until soft peaks form.
4 Strain hot coffee into serving cups; serve topped with rosewater cream.

prep + cook time 15 minutes
makes 1 litre

Glossary

allspice also known as pimento or Jamaican pepper; available whole or ground.

aubergine also known as eggplant. Depending on their age, they may have to be sliced and salted to reduce their bitterness. Rinse and dry well before use.

almonds
blanched skins removed.
flaked paper-thin slices.

buttermilk fresh low-fat milk cultured to give a slightly sour, tangy taste; low-fat yogurt or milk can be substituted.

anchovies small saltwater fish; they are filleted, salted, matured and packed in oil or brine, giving them a characteristic strong taste. Available canned or in jars, they are used in small quantities to flavour a variety of dishes

butternut squash sometimes used interchangeably with the word pumpkin, butternut squash is a member of the gourd family. Various types can be substituted for one another.

caraway seeds a member of the parsley family; available in seed or ground form.

cardamom can be bought in pod, seed or ground form. Has a

distinctive, aromatic, sweetly rich flavour.

cavolo nero a member of the brassica family, this Italian loose-leafed cabbage has very dark green leaves.

chermoulla a Moroccan blend of fresh herbs, spices and condiments, chermoulla is traditionally used for preserving or seasoning meat and fish.

chickpeas also called garbanzos, hummus or channa; an irregularly round, sandy-coloured legume.

chillies available in many types and sizes, both fresh and dried. The smaller the chilli, the hotter it is. Wear rubber gloves when handling chillies, as they can burn your skin. Removing seeds and membranes lessens the heat level.

cinnamon dried inner bark of the shoots of the cinnamon tree. Available as a stick or ground.

coriander also known as cilantro or chinese parsley; bright-green-leafed herb with a pungent flavour. The seeds are also available dried and ground. Ground coriander cannot be substituted for fresh, or vice versa.

couscous a fine, grain-like cereal product, made from semolina.

cumin available both ground and as whole seeds; cumin has a warm, earthy, rather strong flavour.

fennel bulb vegetable, also known as finocchio or anise. Also the name given to dried seeds having a liquorice flavour.

ginger also known as green or root ginger; the thick gnarled root of a tropical plant.

harissa a North African spicy paste made from dried red chillies, garlic, olive oil and caraway seeds. It can be used as a rub for meat, an ingredient in sauces and dressings, or eaten on its own as a condiment. It is available, ready-made, from Middle-Eastern food shops and most supermarkets.

moroccan seasoning a blend of herbs and spices most commonly including cumin, cinnamon and mint. Available in supermarkets, delicatessens and online.

olives
black have a richer and more mellow flavour than the green ones and are softer in texture. Sold either plain or in a piquant marinade.
green those harvested before fully ripened and are, as a rule, denser and more bitter than their black relatives.

orange blossom water concentrated flavouring made from orange blossoms.

paprika ground dried red pepper; available sweet, smoked or hot. Sweet paprika is available at delis, speciality food stores and online.

patty pan squash a small, round variety of squash with a shallow shape and distinctive scalloped edges.

pistachios pale green, delicately flavoured nut inside hard off-white shells. To peel, soak shelled nuts in boiling water about 5 minutes; drain, then pat dry.

pomegranate molasses fresh pomegranate juice reduced to a thick, dark syrup. It has a tangy, fruity flavour. Available in supermarkets, delicatessens and online.

preserved lemon a North African specialty, lemons are preserved, usually whole, in a mixture of salt and lemon juice or oil. To use, remove and discard pulp, squeeze juice from rind, then rinse rind well before slicing thinly. Available from specialty food shops, delicatessens and good supermarkets.

prunes commercially or sun-dried plums.

quince a yellow-skinned fruit with hard texture and astringent, tart taste. Once cooked, they turn a deep-pink-ruby-salmon colour.

ras el hanout a classic Moroccan spice blend often containing more than 20 different spices. The name means 'top of the shop' and is the very best spice blend that a spice merchant has to offer.

rosewater extract made from crushed rose petals; available from health food stores, speciality grocers and good supermarkets.

saffron one of the most expensive spices in the world, true saffron comes only from the saffron crocus, that can produce several flowers a year.

sesame seeds tiny oval seeds available in both black and white varieties; a good source of calcium.

sumac a deep-purple-red astringent spice coarsely ground from berries growing on shrubs that flourish wild around the Mediterranean, sumac adds a tart, lemony flavour to dips and dressings and goes well with poultry, fish and meat. Available from supermarkets, delicatessens and online.

sun-blush tomatoes fresh ripe tomatoes that are placed in the sun to remove almost all of their water content. Not dried for as long as sun-dried tomatoes.

sweet potato fleshy root vegetable with a distinctive orange flesh.

swiss chard also known a silver beet. It has fleshy stalks and large leaves and is prepared in the same way as spinach.

tomato paste triple-concentrated tomato purée used to flavour soups, stews, sauces and casseroles.

turmeric a member of the ginger family, its root is dried and ground; pungent in taste but not hot.

yogurt an unflavoured, full-fat cow's milk yogurt has been used in these recipes unless stated otherwise. Greek yogurt is a thick, creamy variety, traditionally made from ewe's milk.

za'atar a blend of roasted sesame seeds, sumac and crushed dried herbs such as wild marjoram and thyme, its content is largely determined by the individual maker. Used to flavour many familiar Middle Eastern dishes, pizza and savoury pastries; available in delicatessens, specialty food stores and good supermarkets.

Index

A

almonds
almond milk 118
harissa & almond couscous 69
olive & almond couscous 53
apples: green apple & rosewater
milk 117
aubergines
aubergine & pepper with
preserved lemon 111
lamb, aubergine & prune tagine 49

B

beef
beef & bean tagine 29
beef fillet with chermoulla 76
broad beans
broad bean & mint dip 17
tuna tagine with lentils & beans 54
butternut & green been tagine 65

C

cabbage
baked cabbage with tomatoes 108
moroccan chickpea tagine 66
caraway chermoulla prawn skewers
18
carrots
honey-spiced carrots & sweet
potatoes 107
lamb tagine with baby carrots &
olives 42
chermoulla 7, 10, 18
beef fillet with chermoulla 76
chermoulla fish tagine 57
paprika chermoulla 22
chicken
chicken kebabs with blood
orange 21
chicken tagine with fennel &
orange 33
chicken tagine with prunes 34

harissa & orange-roasted chicken
with baby vegetables 75
roast chicken with fruity couscous
stuffing 72
spicy chicken & yogurt tagine 30
chickpeas 7
honeyed lamb tagine 41
lamb tagine with chickpeas 37
lamb tfaya 46
moroccan chickpea tagine 66
olive, chickpea & spinach couscous
salad 100
citrus sparkler 121
coffee, spiced with rosewater cream
122
couscous 8
baked tomato 84
fennel & tomato 88
fruity stuffing 72
harissa & almond 69
herb 58
lamb tfaya 46
lemon 65
minted 79
olive & almond 53
olive & parsley 91
olive, chickpea & spinach salad
100
orange & mint 62
roasted pumpkin & spinach 92
saffron cinnamon 87
with tomato & rocket 95
cumin dressing 92

D

dip, broad bean & mint 17
dressings
cumin 92
moroccan 99
preserved lemon 100
preserved lemon & parsley 104
dukkah 8

E

eggs: lamb tfaya 46

F

fennel
fennel & tomato couscous 88
chicken tagine with fennel &
orange 33
fish see also prawns, sardines, tuna
chermoulla fish tagine 57
crispy spiced fish 22
fast fish tagine 58
white fish & tomato tagine 61

G

grapefruit: citrus sparkler 121
green beans: butternut & green bean
tagine 65

H

harissa paste 8, 11
harissa & almond couscous 69
harissa chermoulla 57
harissa vegetable tagine 62
orange harissa paste 75
honey
honeyed lamb tagine 41
honey-spiced carrots & sweet
potatoes 107
orange honey yogurt 72

K

kidney beans: beef & bean tagine 29

L

lamb
honeyed lamb tagine 41
lamb, aubergine & prune
tagine 49
lamb chops with barley, mint &
cumin 50
lamb, currant & quince tagine 45

lamb kefta tagine 38
lamb tagine with baby carrots &
    olives 42
lamb tagine with chickpeas 37
lamb tfaya 46
lamb with minted couscous 79
sweet potato & lamb shank
    tagine 53
lemons
    citrus sparkler 121
    lemon couscous 65
    lemons, preserved 8, 11, 42, 53, 66
    aubergine & pepper with
        preserved lemon 111
    preserved lemon & parsley
        dressing 104
    preserved lemon dressing 100
    preserved lemon salsa 80
lentils: tuna tagine with lentils &
    beans 54

M
milk
    almond 118
    green apple & rosewater 117
mint
    broad bean & mint dip 17
    citrus sparkler 121
    lamb chops with barley, mint &
        cumin 50
    minted couscous 79
    mint tea 114
    orange & mint couscous 62
    sumac, onion & mint salad 103

O
olives
    lamb tagine with baby carrots &
        olives 42
    olive & almond couscous 53
    olive & parsley couscous 91
    olive, chickpea & spinach couscous
        salad 100
    tomato, olive & radish salad 99
onions
    lamb tfaya
    sumac, onion & mint salad 103
    veal, quince & caramelised onion
        tagine 26

oranges
    chicken kebabs with blood
        orange 21
    chicken tagine with fennel &
        orange 33
    citrus sparkler 121
    moroccan orange & radish salad 96
    orange & mint couscous 62
    orange harissa paste 75
    orange honey yogurt 72

P
pearl barley: lamb chops with barley,
    mint & cumin 50
peppers: aubergine & pepper with
    preserved lemon 111
pomegranate: tomato &
    pomegranate salad 14
prawns: caraway chermoulla prawn
    skewers 18
prunes
    chicken tagine with prunes 34
    lamb, aubergine & prune tagine 49
pumpkin
    roasted pumpkin & spinach
        couscous 92
    sweet pumpkin tagine 69

Q
quinces
    lamb, currant & quince tagine 45
    veal, quince & caramelised onion
        tagine 26

R
radishes
    moroccan orange & radish salad 96
    tomato, olive & radish salad 99
ras el hanout 8, 10
rocket, couscous with tomato & 92
rosewater
    green apple & rosewater milk 117
    spiced coffee with rosewater
        cream 122

S
saffron cinnamon couscous 87
salads
    moroccan orange & radish 96

olive, chickpea & spinach
    couscous 100
sumac, onion & mint 103
tomato & pomegranate 14
tomato & preserved lemon 104
tomato, olive & radish 99
sardines with preserved lemon salsa
    80
spinach
    olive, chickpea & spinach couscous
        salad 100
    roasted pumpkin & spinach
        couscous 92
split peas 8
sumac, onion & mint salad 103
sweet potatoes
    honey-spiced carrots & sweet
        potatoes 107
    sweet potato & lamb shank
        tagine 53

T
tea, mint 114
tfaya 46
tomatoes
    baked cabbage with tomatoes 108
    baked tomato couscous 84
    couscous with tomato & rocket 95
    fennel & tomato couscous 88
    tomato & pomegranate salad 14
    tomato & preserved lemon salad
        104
    tomato, olive & radish salad 99
    white fish & tomato tagine 61
tuna tagine with lentils & beans 54

V
veal, quince & caramelised onion
    tagine 26
vegetables
    harissa & orange-roasted chicken
        with baby vegetables 75
    harissa vegetable tagine 62

YZ
yogurt
    orange honey yogurt 72
    spicy chicken & yogurt tagine 30
za'atar 8

Conversion charts

measures

One metric tablespoon holds 20ml; one metric teaspoon holds 5ml.

All cup and spoon measurements are level. The most accurate way of measuring dry ingredients is to weigh them. When measuring liquids, use a clear glass or plastic jug with metric markings.

We use large eggs with an average weight of 60g.

dry measures

METRIC	IMPERIAL
15g	½oz
30g	1oz
60g	2oz
90g	3oz
125g	4oz (¼lb)
155g	5oz
185g	6oz
220g	7oz
250g	8oz (½lb)
280g	9oz
315g	10oz
345g	11oz
375g	12oz (¾lb)
410g	13oz
440g	14oz
470g	15oz
500g	16oz (1lb)
750g	24oz (1½lb)
1kg	32oz (2lb)

liquid measures

METRIC	IMPERIAL
30ml	1 fluid oz
60ml	2 fluid oz
100ml	3 fluid oz
125ml	4 fluid oz
150ml	5 fluid oz
190ml	6 fluid oz
250ml	8 fluid oz
300ml	10 fluid oz
500ml	16 fluid oz
600ml	20 fluid oz
1000ml (1 litre)	32 fluid oz

length measures

METRIC	IMPERIAL
3mm	⅛in
6mm	¼in
1cm	½in
2cm	¾in
2.5cm	1in
5cm	2in
6cm	2½in
8cm	3in
10cm	4in
13cm	5in
15cm	6in
18cm	7in
20cm	8in
23cm	9in
25cm	10in
28cm	11in
30cm	12in (1ft)

oven temperatures

These are fan-assisted temperatures. If you have a conventional oven (ie. not fan-assisted), increase temperatures by 10–20°.

	°C (CELSIUS)	°F (FAHRENHEIT)	GAS MARK
Very low	100	210	½
Low	130	260	1–2
Moderately low	140	280	3
Moderate	160	325	4–5
Moderately hot	180	350	6
Hot	200	400	7–8
Very hot	220	425	9